A Tribute To ANTONETTE

A Tribute To ANTONETTE
A Collection from Her Early Years

Nancy McDonald

iUniverse, Inc.
New York Lincoln Shanghai

A Tribute To ANTONETTE
A Collection from Her Early Years

Copyright © 2005 by Nancy McDonald

All rights reserved. No part of this book may be used or reproduced by any means, graphic, electronic, or mechanical, including photocopying, recording, taping or by any information storage retrieval system without the written permission of the publisher except in the case of brief quotations embodied in critical articles and reviews.

iUniverse books may be ordered through booksellers or by contacting:

iUniverse
2021 Pine Lake Road, Suite 100
Lincoln, NE 68512
www.iuniverse.com
1-800-Authors (1-800-288-4677)

ISBN-13: 978-0-595-36288-2 (pbk)
ISBN-13: 978-0-595-81081-9 (cloth)
ISBN-13: 978-0-595-80729-1 (ebk)
ISBN-10: 0-595-36288-5 (pbk)
ISBN-10: 0-595-81081-0 (cloth)
ISBN-10: 0-595-80729-1 (ebk)

Printed in the United States of America

Contents

A CUP OF BITTERNESS 1

A DREAM 2

A GYPSY LOVE SONG 3

A LITTLE LONGER 4

A LOVE NEST 5

A LULLABY 6

A PLEA TO THE KIDNAPPERS 7

PLEADING TO LAUGHING EYES 8

AN ABANDONED ROAD 10

AN ACT OF CONTRITION 11

AT THE DANCE 12

AT TWILIGHT 13

ALONE 14

BEAUTY 15

BITTERSWEET 16

BROKEN PROMISES 17

BUDDY BOY OF ALL MY DREAMS 18

CHEERFUL THOUGHTS 19

THE CHILD OF LOVE 20

THE CREATOR OF LOVE 21

CUPID'S BROKEN ARROW 22

DARK HAIR, DARK EYES 23

DEATH 24

THE DIFFERENCE	*25*
THE DREAM ROSE GARDEN	*26*
DREAMS 'NEATH SPANISH SKIES	*27*
DRUM	*29*
EMOTIONS	*30*
FAIRY SPRING	*31*
THE FLOWER FROM MY DARLING'S GRAVE	*33*
GOD'S PRICELESS GIFT	*34*
GONE	*35*
I KNEW	*36*
IF I LOVED YOU	*37*
IN MY SOLITUDE	*38*
IS IT WORTH THE DARE?	*39*
JIMMIE	*41*
JUST A GYPSY LOVE	*42*
JUST A VAGABOND	*43*
KIKI	*44*
LAKE SUPERIOR MOONLIGHT	*46*
LITTLE SISTER	*47*
THE LOCKET ABOVE MY HEART	*48*
LOST HOPES	*49*
LOVE	*50*
LOVE'S COLORS	*56*
ME	*57*
MEMORY ISLAND	*58*
MOODS	*59*
MORE FUN TO MAKE-BELIEVE	*60*
MY COLORADO COWPUNCHER	*62*
MY DAILY PRAYER	*63*

MY LIFE	*64*
MY LOVE	*65*
MY PLEA	*66*
MY ROSARY	*67*
MY SECRET LONGING	*68*
MY SWEETHEART	*69*
NOBODY BUT YOU	*70*
NOT ALWAYS	*71*
ONCE MORE	*72*
ONLY WHEN I DIE	*73*
THE PARTING	*74*
THE PATH ACROSS THE HILL	*75*
THE PHILOSOPHY OF LIFE	*76*
THE PHILOSOPHY OF A THOUGHT	*77*
REGRETS	*78*
REMEMBRANCE	*79*
ROSEBUD	*80*
SCHOOL-DAY MEMORIES	*81*
SMOTHERED FIRES	*82*
STILL MY MARINE	*83*
TALL DREAMS	*84*
THANK YOU FOR SOMETHING SWEET	*86*
TO A DEAR FRIEND	*87*
TO J.M.V.	*88*
TO W.B.	*89*
TO MY MOTHER	*90*
THE TRAIL TO THE NORTHERN PINES	*91*
UNTAMED	*94*
UNTAMED LOVE	*95*

USELESS	97
WHEN I THINK OF YOU	98
WHEN YOU'RE GONE	99
WHY	100
WHY THIS BRIEF STAY CALLED LIFE?	101
WILD DREAMS	103
YESTERDAY	104

A CUP OF BITTERNESS

Love might have brought you all the joys that you craved
All of your hopes and dreams have come true
Love might have brought that inspiration
Of that undaunted ambition in you
There's that unfathomed sparkle in your eyes
Symbolizing romances dear
It seems it has brought you everything
But all it brought me was tears

A DREAM

Out of the night you came;
    It seems I was carried away.
You were so alive, so full of laughter,
Tenderly you held me to you.
You kissed me; it was but a dream,
    But a dream divine,
And shyly, I nestled my head on your shoulder.
I found rest, a rest so tender.
How can I express the peace that stole over me
    As I nestled closer to you?
Why couldn't it go on forever?
It was but a dream,
A treasure, a bit of heaven to give me courage to go on.
How happy joy mingled with tears.
But if you came to me in my darkest hour,
    It's all I want, my darling,
    All that I ask for.
On the altar of love, I offer you my heart,
    My thoughts, a sacrifice divine.

A GYPSY LOVE SONG

Sing to me, my wild gypsy
Sing to me the wild songs of love
Tell me why the wild flowers are blooming
Tell me why the sky is blue above
Where does the wild river lead to?
Where do all the stars go at dawn?
Tell me what the wild winds are whispering
Tell me why the birds sing their song
Did I hear you calling me,
Or am I just dreaming?
If I know you're really calling me
My heart will be singing
Take me with you, my wild little gypsy
My wandering heart is calling out to you
On your wild gypsy trail I'll follow
Just to share this wild love with you

A LITTLE LONGER

If I think a little longer
And feel a little deeper,
I can love the whole wide world.
If I stop and reflect, and look beyond,
And search for the cause, it's seldom wrong.
If I think a little longer
And feel a little deeper,
Things will turn out differently for you.
I wonder if that wasn't what he thought.
He knew if we paused long enough to see all sides,
We would be capable of judging with peace.

A LOVE NEST

If someone asked me what I want
From all the world's splendid things,
It seems I wouldn't ask so very much,
But just one little thing.

A little love nest
Nestled on a crest of a far green hill,
Clustered round with nature's wildwood.
Through the foliage green
Peeps ivory white
Of dainty curtains fluttering in the breeze.
And somewhere beyond ripples the song of falling waters
Draping each haunting strain
Like phantom fingers playing softly on a mandolin.
Then something draws me to the sweet silence
Of an enchanted garden,
Where the perfume of a thousand flowers nodding in the breeze
Send sweet thrills through me.
Then, out from somewhere, I catch a glimpse of you:
The star of my little love nest.

A LULLABY

Sleep, baby, sleep, while mother watches you,
Seeing your eyelids droop with a smile of relief.
Sleep, baby, sleep, while the star shines on high—
Silently darkness creeps, but Mother's always nearby,
Keeping away danger and guarding her little babe,
Silently watching and praying, day after day.

Sleep, baby, sleep, let your dreams wander far and wide,
For always—always—Mother's at your side.
Sleep, baby, sleep—even if your mother's heart is blue,
She's happy, little lamb, knowing that she has you.

You're making her days brighter; the dark clouds are passing away.
You let sunshine through; she glimpses paradise on your baby face.
Your joyous laughter is her laughter, your tears are her tears—
Sleep, baby, sleep, while Mother is singing to you, dear.

A PLEA TO THE KIDNAPPERS

Somewhere a mother's grieving,
A father's brave heart is sad;
All the world is anxiously waiting
For that missing little lad.
God's eyes witnessed that cowardly deed
When out of the night you sneakingly came,
Roughly snatching a sickly, innocent babe
For a few bloody dollars to gain.
Please do not harm his soft, delicate, dimpled limbs;
Do not dim the luster in his laughing blue eyes;
Dampen not the soft, flaxen, curly head,
Or forever still the lips that cry, "Mother."
Empty arms…she once held you close,
Not knowing your fate. Where can you be?
Arms outstretched…her heart is breaking, pleading,
"Bring my little boy back to me."
Oh! What anguish, what sorrow you have brought her.
What frantic grief to a father, a hero who braved death for our country;
Must we bow our heads in disgrace,
Or do we still march on bravely?
You have crushed the hearts of a once-happy home;
You have dishonored our country's cherished name.
All the world pleads: redeem yourself to God and man
By bringing that little boy back again.

PLEADING TO LAUGHING EYES

So wonderful…will I ever forget?
So depthless, so mysterious, dark pools of
Mystic beauty, fathomless…therein lies the
Precious, priceless gift: the lost jewel of my soul
I cannot—yet I dare not—gaze beyond the
Lofty mist…each dark cloud on its journey
Across the deep blue skies imprints a wound
Deep in my heart, its scar never to heal
Dare I go on, knowing the hopelessness
Of life, journeying on to unknown strange places?
Will it hold the sublime wonder in my eyes, or
Will defeat shatter the undaunted courage that
Leads me onward?
Fleeting thrills of bounteous joy unravel
Again across my tired mind…visions that held
Me in its clutches…and unseen hands are leading
Me on…on to far green hills, where golden
Sunshine sprays on scented breezes from crystal
Waters…on, on to where the gypsy birds warble
Their song while winging away 'neath clear blue skies
The lightness of life, the fleeting joys…
Oh! What wondrous delight if I could just go on
Dreaming in my mystic mind to make things real…
Carefree in my gypsy's freedom…on, on to where the
Dusky-purple tints and the ghastly mist comes
Stealing, over the dark walls of high hills
Silhouetted against the quiet starry night…
A voice from out of the darkness keeps calling…
    Calling, like the cry of a lost soul yearning…
        Pleading to someone over yonder, and the gossamer

Web of dreams is brushed rudely aside…and in
My awakening, I find my own heart calling…calling
To you, somewhere beyond

AN ABANDONED ROAD

There is a path now where once there was a road
Where smooth brown earth and jaded rocks
Fell away in deep depression
The trail of wheels and neighing horses and of lighter walks
It grows thick and tall, the grass that was once held at bay
Dared not to rise where tramping feet would crush
But staged on edge where cruel ungainly winds
Vent their wrath unceasingly with rain and dust
It has conquered now, for slowly the grinding ceased
And the lighter steps dwindled with the laughter it had known
It dared to rise between the ruts and bend
To hide the scars from some stray steps that roam
And intrude upon their sanctuary, where conquered winds
Hold not the lash of yore, but with gentleness obey
The lull moods of quiet rains, the brushed air
That shrouds the stillness of an abandoned road

AN ACT OF CONTRITION

Forgive me, lord, for all the wrong this day I've done,
The pain, the sorrow, the sword with which I pierced your sacred heart
Willfully, or unintentionally, not caring of the pangs
I caused you, the agony
You feel for the sheep who have strayed from the flock.
Dear lord, forgive me tonight, and remind me, dear lord of Mount Calvary,
The rough cross stained with your precious blood,
The crown of thorns piercing cruelly your tender head,
And in the gathering darkness, your agonized cry rents the air,
A mortification, for daily I place you on the cross of Mount Calvary.
Forgive me, lord, tonight, and help me, that in the nights to come,
    My sins will be less.

AT THE DANCE

A sea of faces
Dim, shimmering lights
Dancing lightly
Laughing at the taunting melody
Of a song drifting forth
From behind a veil of color and lanterns gay
A song of laughter
A tune of madness
Each tantalizing note
Each throbbing appeal
Pours forth in jest
For but tonight
Arms hold me close
I close my eyes and pretend to feel
The thrill that's lost…Oh, why?
In this sea of faces
Why can't there be
The face I yearn once more to see?

AT TWILIGHT

At twilight, when everything is tranquil and serene,
I steal away and play my melody of broken dreams.
And as it plays on, I watch each star come out,
And like a note, it plays broken memories.
I creep away to hide the tears, and as the last note fades,
There lingers a perfume of love so tender, it pains.
Screening the dullness, the bitterness of the empty years ahead…
For only this fleeting moment, I'll be content.

ALONE

I am alone, now that you're gone
Watching the sun go down
I sit and wait till the moon comes peeping
And till the stars are gleaming
I still wait for you
I pretend you're not far off
Though miles you are from me
When my eyelids close, I feel you near
So near, I feel you kissing me
As the love-lights in my dreams
Shine on your dark hair that gleams
And reflect the deep mystery of your eyes
As they gaze into mine…
I glimpse paradise

BEAUTY

My thoughts of love inspired
By every day's delight
The magic of the sunbeam
And the whispering thrills of night
By a lonely waterfall
I chanced to pass one day,
Upon a bough sat singing
A robin, sweet and gay
I gazed in admiration at
The sheer beauty that God wrought
Song of the breeze and laughing waters
Rippling merrily over the rocks
I hurried on; I could not linger
With this beauty came a wan sadness in my heart
A throb of reconciliation, just beyond…beyond…
I could not linger…I had to go on

BITTERSWEET

I cry because I lost you
Why, I never had you, darling
The feel of your hand upon mine
The thrill of a stolen kiss
Are just make-believes I secretly treasure
But in reality, not even a smile
No, not even a remembrance
Still, I go on pretending, dreaming of you
Like today, tomorrow will be the same
But the nights will be mine…to go on
Pretending, dreaming of you
Forever, darling…always loving you

BROKEN PROMISES

The hours I spent with you
Are moments that now make me blue
Why did we ever go apart?
Why are you always in my heart?
Every minute of each day
Makes me yearn just to say
Are you still remembering me?
Every night that has passed
Makes me yearn for the last
When you kissed me so tenderly
Why, I never knew it would end so soon
Why did you promise to love me always?
Was it some other's eyes that were brighter than mine
That led you away from me?
Why, there's not a one in this world
Not another girl
That could love you as I loved you

BUDDY BOY OF ALL MY DREAMS

I'm always dreaming of you, Buddy Boy;
I'm always longing for you, Buddy Boy.
You bring the sunshine in my dreams;
You bring gladness in my heart,
Buddy Boy of all my dreams.

What is the sunshine without you?
What good are raindrops when you're gone?
It's like the moonbeams on a deserted beach,
Buddy Boy of all my dreams.

Happy days without you cannot be,
Because birdies don't sing on the old apple tree—
They miss you as much as I do,
Buddy Boy of all my dreams.

You're like the sunshine to the flowers,
You're like the raindrops to the fields,
You're like the moonbeams on a darkened beach,
You're like heaven to me,
Buddy Boy of all my dreams.

CHEERFUL THOUGHTS

Why count the hours that are slipping away?
Why count the lonely days?
Why count the weeks that are drifting by?
Why count the tears and sighs?
They just add up in this drama of life
Unwanted heartaches and tears
If we but forget the unhappy thoughts
Of doubting fates and fears
If we instead count the happy hours
That are spent with friends that are true
If our thoughts linger on happy memories
We won't be feeling blue
There are two heartaches to each smile
Two lonely hours spent to each happy one
If we but look ahead and think of pleasant things
Life won't be such a hard road to travel

THE CHILD OF LOVE

The child of love is nearly always unwanted,
Despised, and uncared for, and is sometimes left
To go the pathways of life alone amongst strangers,
    Unloved, unknown, unwanted.
It was love that gave him existence,
Yet mother's love is denied him.
His soft, delicate features reflect the image, the beauty,
    The music of the soul
When unselfish love has known its heights,
Yet it's unwanted—
The purest, the sweetest, the tenderest of all—
The child of love.

THE CREATOR OF LOVE

Jesus, the creator of love divine,
The supremacy of his devotion, his constant thought,
From his birth to his cruel death upon the cross
Was for us—he gave this love sublime.

He showed us by his sacrifice
The meekness and sadness on his divine face,
The beauty of his soul that was not hidden,
And the torture and sorrow he endured.
It was love for us that led him to perform numerous miracles;
It was for love for us
That he bravely went to his death.
Lord, he gave in abundance.
Oh! How beautiful, how precious that gift: love.

CUPID'S BROKEN ARROW

Darting from somewhere
Piercing my heart
Its wound opened
Showing without
Cupid's arrow
My hand upon it
I thrusted it forth
I found the point gone
Left in my heart
Cupid's arrow
I held it tightly
And gazed in your eyes
And found why the arrow's point
Was left in my heart
You smiled as I aimed it at you
It went straight at your heart
Then dropped heavily to the ground
It failed to do its part
Cupid's broken arrow

DARK HAIR, DARK EYES

Dark hair, dark eyes
Under pale starry skies
Lend a picture of enchanting paradise
Throbbing hearts and honey-spoken words
Fading in the gloom
'Neath the tender moon
Caressing eyes and blinding tears
A little wisp of the breeze
Draws you to me
What night of night could I love you more
Then tonight, your dark head on my breast
In a sleep of heavenly rest
Creeping so slowly, soft white fingers to my lips
A touch…a thrill…then crushing you to me
For a moment of happiness…so tenderly

DEATH

Death: an adventure to go through, like that of life
The body from which the soul has parted lies not forever in its grave of night
The soul is free…it goes and it achieves its goal far greater
than that which in life was only a mystery
Thick veils of darkness are brushed rudely aside
This unknown universe is pierced through by the phantom eyes of death
Leaving the naked truth flashing across our tired minds
Astonishing us beyond…all forgotten ambitions surge through us
The pathways are clear to go on to accomplish our aim
Knowing we will succeed if we but have the courage to go on

Death: the grim weeper of life
Death: the freedom of our souls

THE DIFFERENCE

I got up early one morning,
And rushed right into the day;
I had so much to accomplish
That I didn't have time to pray.

Problems just tumbled about me,
And heavier came each task.
Why didn't God help me?
I wondered; he answered, "You didn't ask."

I wanted to see joy and beauty,
But the day toiled on gray and bleak.
I wondered why God didn't show me;
He said, "You didn't seek."

I tried to come into God's presence;
I used all my keys at the lock.
God gently and lovingly chided,
"My child, you didn't knock."

I woke up early this morning,
And paused before entering the day;
I had so much to accomplish,
But I had to take time to pray.

THE DREAM ROSE GARDEN

I might wander in a dream rose garden
Its magic spell scented with the rarest rose
And I might be lost in its dreamlike splendor
I won't be lonely if I know
That somewhere beyond those shadowy bushes
I might wander and come to you
To find you bending over the rarest rose
The one I meant for you

DREAMS 'NEATH SPANISH SKIES

What does it matter if you love me or not
If the treasure I thought mine is lost?
I can pretend I'm under Spanish skies again
Listening to the mad love coming out of the night
Pouring forth from the strains of a guitar
Swaying in dreams on romantic nights
Closer the music comes, till from haunting eyes
And from scarlet lips…
The sweet rippled music of love
Under Spanish skies, I learned to love you
My gypsy wandering in breathless dreams
Come to me, O love, I'm waiting
Together we'll wander in dreams
Come to me, oh love, I'm lonely
Listen to the yearnings of my heart
Oh, beautiful, thy mysterious eyes are longing for me
Though fringed in darkness, my heart can see
Your faded red rose on your ear is falling
Your sweet red lips no more are smiling
Oh, my love, under this pale moon I've waited
Pouring my love forth to your deafness's ears
Calling to you, longing for you, I've waited
Till your soft footsteps again I felt near
Listen to me, O love, you're lonely
From my garden of dreams I've found this rose
In your raven hair, upon your lily-white ear
I long to fasten it there
Oh, my love, under Spanish skies I've built these dreams
In this lovely spot, where only your eyes can see
Though far away, you didn't forget to remember

You heard me in your dreams and came back to me.
Oh, my love, to you I give my all
My love, my longing, my life for you
Come with me, or take me with you, darling
For without you, I cannot linger on

DRUM

I love the drum of the roaring waves
I love the million lights that flicker, then fade away
I love the wild song the soft wind's singing,
I love the sweet-scented breezes around me winging
I love them all…for it means you

EMOTIONS

These overtures of love
They are the fabric of dreams
The color of romances
And the still, sweet smile on Death's face
Death, the end of misery
The numbing of pain
And the freedom of our souls
Beyond then, we do not surmise
Just pretending…heavenly divine
Ambitions flare…hopes run high
And doubts are cast aside
On, on to another being: our true self
Not to conquer, not to lead
But to be led on forever…by one divine

FAIRY SPRING

O Fairy Spring, stay away a little longer
Do not come taunting me with your laughing eyes
Your chirping birds, your budding trees, your
    blooming flowers, your skies of blue
O Fairy Spring, stay away till I'm prepared for you
Let me first build an armor that you can't penetrate
With your enchanting gadgetry, dancing up to me unawares
Until I find the portals broken and your fairy feet crushing
The heart I tried to keep from breaking when you left
For you will not bring back all that Autumn's harvest has taken away
You bring a cup of bitterness in your fairy hands instead
And your magic wand will only light up each throb of pain I've tried
    to still
Stay away, O Fairy Spring, don't taunt me with your bewitching ways
Do not weave a spell around me showing me paradise lost
Don't wake up the old pain that cold winter snows have tried to hide
O Fairy Spring, be merciful to me
I've loved you other years, when you came waking up the flowers
The trees, the green grass that slumbered 'neath Winter's white snows
Your feet dancing along lightly, calling, calling
And always in my heart there was an answering chord
Renewing lost hopes, catching the lightness of your mood
    until you found me following you
And always when you left, you pressed a kiss lightly on my
    cheek…until at last I found
O Fairy Spring, you betrayed me, you flitted away, lightly clutching
In your fairy hands the priceless jewel you stole from me
How could you be so cruel and still so beautiful, so serene?

Stay away, Fairy Spring, stay away till Winter snows claim me
And into that far land where you left my loved one, let me first go

THE FLOWER FROM MY DARLING'S GRAVE

Drenched from the tears of a broken heart
Mellowed by the blood-red tints of dawn
Kissed by the fairies that steal into the night
The flower from my darling's grave

More precious than jewels of the earth
As dear as life's dream
The treasure pressed close to my heart
The flower from my darling's grave

It was just a little flower, once so bright
Now its petals' edges dried and brown
Its little life crushed, its heart is dead
But it's the flower from my darling's grave

It grew alone there, so sweet and bright
Braving the wind and storm
A voice from out of nowhere whispered:
"Take it, my love, it's yours alone"

GOD'S PRICELESS GIFT

Moonlight, youth's inspiration
Freedom in reverie…love's glorification
Ecstasy in love, binding two human souls
Symbolize that great unknown: love
Defy it? No one can acknowledge its meaning
Each individual interprets it with his own instinct
Love, seen through the eyes of youth
Mysteriously, yet it harmonizes with their souls
They see not the color of the eyes
For the eyes are the windows of the soul
But they see therein something sweet!
Divine…as God meant love to be
Hearts beat to the tune, the music of the soul
Surrenders at last to youth
God's priceless gift…love

GONE

Gone from my arms you are tonight
Alone in my dreams and tears
Years cannot dim the magic of the night
That held for me in other years
Somehow I don't want to forget you
Still there come times I do
If love had never come to me
I wouldn't now feel so blue
Alone I am watching each day passing
Each day passing in a gloom
Yet there remains the sweetest of memories
Of that other year, that other day in June

I KNEW

They were the steps I used to climb
And now that I can fly, I have no need
The wire hand that shaped our beginning
Knew we had to reach out before we could feel within
As tangible as our earthly being
The budding need to entice our outer senses
A tale of a life unfolding
A pattern to awakening
A seed in my primal being
It was a story told at my mother's knee
I knew love that strained at the outer edges
I knew sorrow that broke the bottomless pit

IF I LOVED YOU

If I loved you
Time and again I would try to say
All I want you to know
If I loved you

Words wouldn't come in an easy way
Round in circles
Longing to tell you, but afraid and shy
I'd let my golden chances pass me by
You would leave me
Off you would go in the mist of day
Never, never to know

How I loved you—if I loved you

IN MY SOLITUDE

In my solitude, I have lived a life with you
With days of happiness and nights of peace and rest
In my solitude, I watched our love grow old
And in every glance there was romance retold
I feel your tender arms around me still
I feel your sweet lips pressing mine
I still remember all the things you whispered
Even though it's been such a long time
In my solitude, I can hear the music playing
And the words are saying, "I love you"
In my solitude, let me drift again
Where I'll be content, in solitude with you

IS IT WORTH THE DARE?

Life, what is your meaning?
I tried to understand—but somehow, I failed.
You are so beautiful in all your enchanting ways,
But underneath, there's a cruelty that pains.
You symbolize youth's adventurous spirit
With beautiful moods 'neath a mask of deceit,
Then you take those precious dreams and crush them,
And leave but a grim knowledge of the merciless reality.
You keep on taking, but you never give;
You bring on pain, but you will not heal.
You show your merciless strength,
Knowing it's beyond our human hearts to feel.
With heartless determination, you dare to keep on
Hiding 'neath this dreadful cloak of beauty.
Is there a reckoning somewhere beyond,
Where it will be torn aside, exposing your mockery?
There is a challenge in all your undertakings,
But you taunt us if we try to go the way;
For every step ahead, a wound you meanly inflict,
Or with false promising, you lead us astray.
Life, you challenge my reckless moods;
Your jeers are but spurs to lead me on.
And should I find, at dusk, I'm crushed and broken,
There will be new courage to lead me at dawn;
There will be a false gaiety—how could it otherwise be?
Your taunts will be met with grim determination,
And I'll build my dreams in spite of defeat,
If only in my vagabond imagination,
A moment's joy and an endless sorrow.
Your cost is beyond all compare;

The struggle is long without victory—
I sometimes wonder if it's worth the dare.

JIMMIE

Nothing matters now
Nothing rhymes
Nothing harmonizes
Just an emptiness, a vacant space
Beauty…Oh! I must not think of beauty
There is no beauty left…nothing
Not even dreams
I see a vague space…fleecy clouds
Just beyond, beyond…something dark in the distance
Moving closer…closer
Oh! What anguish, what sorrow
No, no, what wondrous delight, what beauty
For it's you…you…calling me…calling me

JUST A GYPSY LOVE

It was a gypsy love I gave you,
Wild, impulsive, but true;
I ripped down all standards, for I didn't understand
This gypsy heart of mine, unheedingly
     went on loving recklessly—
It was the only way it knew.
It built its own code…and that was freedom—
A reckless smile for others that disapproved.
Didn't stop to think, to realize
     it was too reckless to go on,
For this gypsy heart of mine knew no other way to love.

I picked the choice words and wove them into a verse;
I thought up the gayest name I knew,
Then wrapped them up in wings of love.
I sent them all to you.
I waited a long time…then slowly, the wild light in my eyes dimmed,
The wild song in my heart stilled.
My reckless gypsy love was not returned.

But stubbornly, I would not show defeat;
I gallantly went on pretending…pretending.
Somehow that image in my dreams became a reality.
I closed my heart to all others;
A fantastic song again came from my yearning heart,
But it's a haunting taunting melody that came echoing back…hollow.

JUST A VAGABOND

I tried to put you out of my heart
And take another in
But I couldn't play the part
I failed in the end
On my way I'll go
Just a vagabond

Without ties or home
And not knowing where I'm bound
'Cause you made me what I am
Just a vagabond

KIKI

Kiki, she's a dandy little pal, Kiki
She's the sweetest little gal, Kiki
You've got to know her to love her
She will make you laugh and play
She will chase the blues away
That's Kiki
She's in heaven when she's happy
She's in hell when she's blue
There are no in-betweens for Kiki
But she's the gamest pal you ever knew
Oh, Kiki
She doesn't get jealous
And she doesn't get sore
She doesn't tell a feller
That he makes her bored
'Cause it's Kiki
She knows the sweetest way to kiss
And she'll give you a demonstration
She knows a good deal about love
'Cause that was her education
Oh, you ought to know Kiki
She'll never win a prize for beauty
With her flying curly hair
And her shape might knock Ziegfeld cold
But who cares, as long as it's Kiki?
In her life, she never did anything right
She says things out of place
But she's sorry if she makes you unhappy
And the tears runs down her face,
Sad, sad Kiki

She's a truthful little trooper, that Kiki
And a great big spitfire too
But after all's said and done, she's a dandy runt
That'll never make a minute blue
Three cheers for Kiki

LAKE SUPERIOR MOONLIGHT

Down by the shores of Lake Superior,
There hums the song of the roaring waves;
'Neath a golden moon gleaming on crystal waters
Strays a wisp of perfumed breezes rare.
Through the veil of darkness creeps a haunting strain
Of swaying trees somewhere beyond;
And the dark waters rippling over the sands
Set my soul free to go on and on.

I catch again the priceless magic of the night,
The freedom that the roaring waters call;
Imprisoned, now free to go on,
Where unseen hands are leading me, beyond, beyond.
Magic waters, in your grip you have my soul;
You lead me on to mysterious places;
Forgetting, and leaving all behind,
My soul rises up to meet my fleeting thoughts—
On, on to reach my goal.

LITTLE SISTER

Ah! Little sister, how I long for you
    When underneath the twinkling stars
Ah! Little sister, how I yearn for you
    Though you are gone and ever so far
Though sometimes I feel you near me
    Your joyous voice it seems I hear
Your little heart seems bubbling with life again
Dear little sister, could it be real?
There come nights when I see you clearly
    With your little babies you always loved
They go joyfully trailing around you
    Like the angels that come from above
They are happy to have you with them
    And I know that you're happy too
For your sweet, joyful face seems never to be sad
    And in my dreams, I know you are glad
A trail of tears you left behind you
    When you flew to the land beyond
Where angels came down to greet you
    And welcomed you with a joyful song
I'm glad that you're happy, little sister
    Up there, where you don't feel any pain
Where you forget that you've ever been
    In the vale of tears…for heaven to gain

THE LOCKET ABOVE MY HEART

Years have passed between us
    Since the day we went apart;
There is something that I'll remember:
    The locket above my heart.
A little thing, but oh, so dear,
    With a chain that's made of gold;
It's still the sparkling, precious thing
    That it was on that day of old.
It opens up its little face
    And shows its radiant jewel:
A smiling face that is so dear
    And a curl I took from you.
Though the years are long and lonely,
    And the pathways are dark,
There is something that will lead me onward—
    The locket above my heart.

LOST HOPES

Watching each raindrop falling
    Against the window pane
They are like teardrops falling
    From my eyes in vain
They're like rainbow-colored diamonds
    Flashing brilliant lights
Splashing against the window
    Then disappearing from sight
Gazing out into the gloomy mist
    At the dark clouds in the sky
Weariness engulfs me
    As my thoughts stray far and wide
Unknowingly gazing beyond
    While my eyes are brimming with tears
As through the milky whiteness
    Your familiar face appears

LOVE

With your love and trust
I transcend myself
Different heights command my spirit
Whose subterranean base knows no fear
And I glory in its untold variation of lilting tone

An unheard-of symphony
My mind becomes void of the pull of earth
For it's filled with the unending realm of joy
And mirrors in my face the beauty
For one moment I remember you
From my height I bring my lighted gaze down
Grasping your hand; you glide up to my bosom
And together the veil parts
And we are immersed in what love is

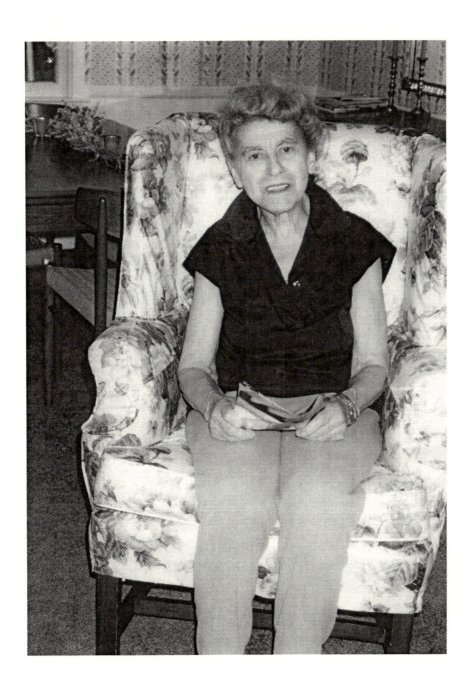

LOVE'S COLORS

I wish I could paint a picture of the love I had for you
There wouldn't be jabs of colors, but tints of softest hues
I would use a bit of yellow and the softest tints of green
The magic color purple woven in my tapestry of dreams
Pink I would not forget, for its color's sheen is youth,
And entwined I'll also put a pastel shade of blue
It would be like a rainbow, that picture of my dreams
Blue and gold and amber shades and silvery sheens

ME

You gave me eyes that twinkle, like moonlight on the sea
Its darkness enchants its depthless light, like a jewel so rarely
They're guarded with long lashes, shaded in dark delight
They sometimes are so haunting and sometimes are so bright

My soul reflects through them and shows what's in my heart
That's why nobody wants me: they all seem to want to part
They all seem wild about me, when first we chance to meet
They gaze into my eyes and loudly appraise me

They love to twine their fingers through my soft and silky hair
They mess it up and it tumbles down—they don't seem to care
They say my hair is beautiful, so soft and full of lights
Its natural wave is rippling in the breezes of the night

I listen eagerly, drinking in all their words of praise
But down deep in my heart, I know they will not stay
Still no sorrow do I feel, because I do not care
I just seem to want to drift along; it doesn't matter where

MEMORY ISLAND

You were so sweet and wonderful
    How I long to be with you
Like in those bygone moments of yesterday
    Underneath the pale, silvery moon
I can still hear the tinkle of your laughter
    I can still see your starry eyes
We sat side by side, just dreaming
    With your little hand clasped in mine
We talked a lot of sweet nothings
    Planning our future, we two
But fate took a hand and parted us
    That's why I'm lost to you
It might be for the best that we parted
    Going our separate ways
But oh, how my heart is aching
    When the sun sets each day
You were so sweet and wonderful
    That's why I can't forget you
Those promises we made I still remember
    That's why I'm lonely and blue
I wonder where you are tonight
    Do you remember with tears in your eyes?
Like that day long ago I can't forget
    When we two said good-bye

MOODS

The lie your firm, red lips whispered
Your dark, laughing eyes that have deceived
Would I but have the power to brush away
Each false, lingering memory
You chose to break the link that bound me
To a heart that proved not true
Shattered all my dreams about me
Still not the love I have for you
Stripped of all…still I'll go on
Till vague is the memory of you
Should moments come when my mind shall stray
I'll try and lead it away from you

MORE FUN TO MAKE-BELIEVE

I try to smile and I try to be
Something the world wants and still satisfy me
My pretended smile is but a mask
To hide the while the bitter task
Why pretend? One cannot play
Two roles at one time and still get away
I must leave one; I cannot have both
I shall pursue the one that means the most
In dreams, I found life is so sweet
In real life, there are too many heartaches to meet
I can imagine adventures that start
And I'm bound to play the leading part
And if there'll come a time I'll regret
There won't be any sorrow, no one loses a bet
For if my dreams crumble, there is no one to see
Just how it matters, how it's hurting me
I'll borrow Aladdin's lamp and go to where?
The places that good girls don't dare
In a wild encampment around gypsy fires
I'll dance with madness, my one desire
A vagabond serenading me
His songs of madness—so thrilling it'll be
And should I succumb to his laughing eyes
I know that no one will ever be wise
I'll sing my wild songs; I need not fear
For only my vagabond will ever hear
I'll thrill to his kisses 'neath starlit skies
And listen in rapture to his countless lies
(You wouldn't think I'd ever believe
Even in dreams, what the gypsies tell me)

And if I tire and want to be
Something far different than a wild gypsy
On to another place, my vagabond heart
Ready in a jiffy to play another part
If I want to be a princess or a queen
On a throne of make-believe, that's where I'll be seen
There's no bonds to hold me, no matter how strong
I can laugh or I can cry my whole life long
Why be tied down to realities?
There is more fun in make-believe

MY COLORADO COWPUNCHER

I have a lonesome cowboy
    Who rides the Western plains
In a little county in Colorado
    Where the sun's as hot as flames,
You'll hear him in the morning
    Just at the break of day
A-ropin' and a-shootin'
    As he rides his great big bay
Oh! He's the Colorado cowpuncher
    A-singin' all the time.
He tells me he is lonesome
    When the sun begins to shine
Ah! Don'cha believe, boys
    He's allus tellin' lies
When he says he's awful lonely
    He's not, and I'll tell you why
He counts the days till payday
    When the boss forks him some dough
For then you'll see him sneakin'
    To town, where he's bound to go
It's there he starts to gamblin'
    His payday all away
And then he says he's lonesome
    When he writes to me next day

MY DAILY PRAYER

I place my life in your hands, O Jesus
And may everything I do be pleasing to you
Whichever path you choose, I'll follow
Whatever burden you give me, I'll bear it
Only be near me when shadows creep
Over the rough roads of life, where temptation lurks
Let me gaze upon your divine face with a shameless spirit
Knowing in my heart that I've done my best
I know that is all that you ask of me
All that you want from this brief trail called life
So help me, Jesus, to do what's right

MY LIFE

Was that all life's gift to me:
Tears and a broken heart?
I don't see why they picked on me
To play this unwanted part
Are my dreams forever to be broken?
Am I always to share them alone?
Is life only to beat and crush me?
I dare not ask, for now I know

MY LOVE

Heart of my heart
Soul of my soul
It was love we both knew
Which never grows old
Since the day you first thought me to care
How wonderful you were, how beautiful and fair
Can you remember, dear, that evening near the stream?
How I told you of my love and hopes and dreams?
How you ran your soft fingers through my hair
And whispered that you too loved and cared?
Can you remember, dear, how happy I was?
How I pressed you to my heart and kissed your lips
While softly you murmured sweet words to me?
Heart of my heart
Soul of my soul
I'll always love you
As I did of old

MY PLEA

No more tears will I shed for you
No more heartthrobs will I feel
For the last flood of tears came last at twilight
When on my knees to God, I prayed this appeal

O God, grant me the courage to go on
This agony is more than I can bear
His unwilling heart I do not ask
But only to forget

His laughing eyes that twinkled so merrily
His smile that was never meant for me
His nearness that only brought pain and uncertainty
And his name that is forever on my lips

MY ROSARY

The cloudless sky is rosy tonight
    As thoughts of romance flip across my tortured mind;
It lives again the years that have gone by,
    And I find a bleeding heart whose wound is opened wide.
Across bright pathways of years now dim,
    My weary mind often strays;
I retrace each step with mournful tread,
    For on my heart a cross is laid.
I will try to carry it bravely on,
    Each tear a star that shines
To brighten a path that once was dim,
    For you, sweetheart, mine.
Each breath a prayer from grieving lips,
    Each thought of love that knows no end—
I kiss each bead and try to understand
    That someday you and I will meet again.

MY SECRET LONGING

Someone to care
I've longed for someone to love me
Someone who would care where I went
What I did
And what I thought
Someone who would think of me
And love me
Day after day
Week after week
Until weeks became years
My heart was aching with longing
For someone who would give me a love that would last
I loved because I wanted love
My whole heart gave out love
I was hungry for someone to care
All through the days and nights
That terrible loneliness and that overwhelming desire
For someone who would love me in return
I needed someone who understood me
Without being told
Who cared without being asked to care
And whose love was true
I found you, darling
But you went away

MY SWEETHEART

There are tears in your eyes, my sweetheart.
    You're sorry that I'm leaving you.
Let me kiss away your tears, sweetheart,
    And do not feel so blue.
I'll be dreaming of you, sweetheart—
When the light of day fades away
    It'll make me blue.
There will be a star shining, sweetheart,
On that starry dome that will lead me home to you.
All cares shall vanish and skies turn blue
    When I'm coming back, sweetheart—
Coming back to you.

NOBODY BUT YOU

Nobody's arms brought me contentment
Nobody's kisses thrilled me through
Nobody's nearness dazed me completely
Nobody, until I met you
Then all of a sudden, the world was brighter
All of a sudden, the skies were blue
All of a sudden, my heart felt lighter
Honey, it's because I met you

You seem to make me feel I am in heaven
Seems I hear the angels singing low
If this is the way you feel when you're in heaven
Honey, do not ever from me go
For what could I do without you?
How could I ever get along
Now that you've taught me what love can do?
Don't leave me, or I'm gone

NOT ALWAYS

I'm not asking for always
I know it's too much from you
But give me an evening
Beneath the moon, near the blue lagoon
Where I can tell you of my yearnings
Lay your head upon my breast
Let my lips rest on your hair
And sing…I want you to sing for me
Let us pretend to be sweethearts
If only for an evening

ONCE MORE

Wake up, my love:
>The morning sun shines brightly above
>With fleeting feet and laughing eyes
>Let's romp away with the song of the breeze
>Wake up, my love, and follow me

Wake up, my love:
>The noonday tide is passing by
>From the lake not far away
>Can't you hear the songs of the waves calling?
>Wake up, my love, do not stay

Wake up, my love:
>The moon is dripping its beams of light
>There are hidden shadows playing here and there
>And gypsy fairies singing love songs that we knew
>Wake up, my love, I need you

ONLY WHEN I DIE

I might forget the magic of your smile
    The color of your fluffy hair
The liquid pools of your laughing eyes
    Where love was shining there
I might forget that darling dimple
    Every time your lips would smile
And the dazzling beauty of your pearly teeth
    That would flash every little while
Then I might forget the roses on your cheeks
    That nature planted there
And in her mysterious way, she also put
    The sunshine in your hair
And if I do forget these all
    You'll know it's not my fault
For not even death could make me forget
    The sweetest one of all

THE PARTING

Let's linger here a moment longer
Unseen…stealing on to the lake
Where the gleaming moon lightly
Dances over the dark shimmering waters
Into some deep preclude
As if by magic, the twilight veils and hides the pain
And hushes the whispering winds, the sobs
As if they feel this brief hour too sacred to intrude
It steals away, and in the distance it forms a guard
The misty gloom gathers around, as if, in pretence, a barrier from the cruel reality
This last mad hour, crowd in the years of love that's lost
To give me heart in some unguarded moment
I might forget to smile
Its bitter memories remembering
Hold me tight in your arms, dear heart
And forget for a moment the dawn
Kiss me as if the parting was for a brief space
And whisper words that in this lost garden
I might come in after years and find solace in its sweet silence
And the dim echo of tonight will give me courage to go on
Feeling once more your sweet presence
With a gust of wind lightly pressing a kiss from your phantom lips

THE PATH ACROSS THE HILL

There's a little path that winds its way
Across those purple hills
It will lead you to a certain place
Where it's lonely and still
It's the place I used to go
With someone at my side
It breaks my heart when I think of it
And tears fills my eyes
It's long since I tramped on it
When the sky seemed a brighter blue
The birds sang more sweetly
When I used to walk with you
I have not been there since that day
When we were sweethearts still
But someday I shall tread again
The path across the hill

THE PHILOSOPHY OF LIFE

If we but tore aside the curtains of make-believe
And exposed the heart of its soul-stirring anxiety
We would find a mess of shattered hopes and broken dreams
A deluge of emotion too great to comprehend
Blindly we go on, masking each sorrow
Hiding each pain behind a smile
Grasping a moment of happiness today
Only to pay for it tomorrow
Tear aside life's curtain of mystery
For a moment you'll know its soul
Its travail, its dreadful beauty, its infinite sadness, its merciless strength
Grimly, we try to understand
But it's far beyond the power of humans' finite minds to grasp
This meaning of earthly existence—that its ending is only death

THE PHILOSOPHY OF A THOUGHT

If one could put together each fragment that the mind
Seems to grasp but for an instant, then vanish
To fashion out and mold for some future use
From some dark, past a vague light that once puzzled
Save each bit, each fragment in some locked place
One might find a meaning of a thought

It comes to us when blinded by some image dulling our keener sense
Only to find its presence an instant too late
We try to follow, but it's useless; it has left but a mere shadow
Yet too blurred to understand, we ponder for awhile
And taunting us, it comes back, only to slip away again
Firing our imagination until we build something entirely different

What a joke it seems that one can't conquer the mind
To command it, to lead it on where one will
But it stands the opposite; the soul commands the body
And the soul belongs to God.

For each good thought is a seed that God has sown,
And sometimes sown on barren soil
Only to wilt and die
For a good seed to take root in one's mind, it must first banish all others
And cultivate a place where only good thoughts may develop

REGRETS

I wish I could turn back the years
And build over yesterday's dreams
Where shadows creep, I'll brighten it with sleep
Then there wouldn't be any wasted dreams
If I had known what I know now…
Now that those tender dreams have died
I would have laughed at life, not dreaming of tomorrow
Every little hour I would live like a flower
Smiling, heedless of deaths tomorrow

REMEMBRANCE

I took away a sweet remembrance
    Of laughing eyes twinkling merrily,
Your waving hand saying farewell—
    Had I but known it was the last to be.
As the months sped by, I grew lonely;
    I yearned to be back with you, sweetheart,
But I braved it through, for in my heart I thought
    My reward would be you, sweetheart.
Your name was forever on my lips;
    Your laughing eyes, gazing through the mist,
Were something sacred to me.
    I seem to feel you near me,
Guiding me on and on;
    Alas, I knew how much you meant to me,
Sweetheart, sweetheart of mine.
    But God didn't mean it to be
In reality, this love sublime,
    For one bright day, he called you away,
Sweetheart, and left me behind.

ROSEBUD

You came and went
Still there lingers a part of you
You're like a song that's stilled
Its melody lingers on

You're like a rosebud in the shadow
Hiding somewhere in the night
You know it's there, scented everywhere

I know you're there, but I cannot see
How like the rosebud in the evening

SCHOOL-DAY MEMORIES

School-day memories
They all come back to me
Where are my school-day pals?
Where are my school-day gals?
School-day memories

Is it now like it used to be?
How I do wish I could return
Just once more, to study and learn
Though I'll never tread on the schoolhouse floor
And my hand shall never touch its door
My treasure they shall ever take from me
Of those beautiful school-day memories

SMOTHERED FIRES

You gazed into my eyes so long ago
It seems but like yesterday
I tried to close my heart and forget
For like a star, you're so far away
You went away and stayed so long
The yearning in my heart was stilled
I thought that I had forgotten you
Until I gazed in your eyes again
How can I tell you the hopeless tears,
The hidden love that in my heart remained
Through all these gloomy and painful years,
Only to come back to life again?
I must not care, for it will only leave
A wound that time would never heal
I pray that our path shall not cross again
And let this love for you be in memory sealed

STILL MY MARINE

I have a pal whom I've never met
    He sails the ocean blue
There are times when I do think of him
    When the stars are scarce and few
He does not know that I love him so
    Or care in any way
But somehow, he shall never know
    How I yearn for him each day
He told me once that his ideal
    Was a girl with curly hair
With dark brown eyes that sparkle
    That brings sunshine everywhere
I played with him, because I knew
    The girl of his dreams was I
I knew he felt bad, but I was glad
    I was living in paradise
But let me tell you the saddest news
    That comes from the hand above
My pal has found another one
    A girl he does not love.
He told me that he loved me true
    And always will I be
The little girl of sunshine
    And beautiful memories.
Oh! My heart cries out for him
    Though his face I've never seen
But now he belongs to someone else
    But still he's my Marine

TALL DREAMS

What lies beyond the rolling hills
    Beyond the forest of trees
Beyond the snow-capped mountains
    And beyond the sky-blue sea?
I often dream and wonder where
    The end of the rainbow disappears
Beyond somewhere, in some far-off place
    I dream it's there I fear
I wish I had a four-wheel Ford
    That travels at top speed
That needs no fixes, needs no punchers
    Or gas and oil to feed
You'll hear of me a-goin' far
    Beyond the hills and forest of trees
I'll park my Ford and the mountains climb
    And gaze out longingly at the sea.
I might get a lonesome feeling
    As often I get that way
When all the places on land I've seen
    I'd want to go some other place someday.
So why not get an airplane
    With an engine that never goes wrong?
In rain or fog or storm it'll go
    And it'll give it pep as I sing a song.
Of course Lindy was the first bird
    Who flew alone across the sea,
The crowd in Paris cheered him high
    And crowned him the "Lone Eagle" of the sky
He deserves it all, and even more
    For it was a deed of yesterday

But wait till all my dreams come true
    When my plane and I hop off someday
We will travel up above the clouds
    High up till we reach the stars
For we would like to hear the angels sing
    It will guide us on our journey far.
In some far-off place where nobody's been
    I'll bring my plane to a landing stop
There will be no one around to cheer me
    But a few trees here and there and a pile of rock
I know the folks out here won't believe me
    That I've been to no-man's land
'Cause there was no one around to cheer me
    As when Lindy in Paris did land
But I'll surprise them all by bringing something from far
    The place they say I've never been
I'll look high and low till I find it
    The gold at the rainbow's end.

THANK YOU FOR SOMETHING SWEET

Throw me a kiss from across the room
Say I look nice when I'm not
Touch my hair as you cross my chair
Little things mean a lot

Give me your arm as we cross the street
Call me at six on the dot
Don't have to buy me diamonds and pearls
Champagne or such
I never cared for diamonds and pearls
And honestly, honey, they just cost money

Give me your hand when I've lost the way
Give me your shoulder to cry on
Whether the day is bright or gray
Give me your heart to rely on
Give me the warmth of your secret smile

Show me that you haven't forgot
For now and forever
For always and ever
Little things mean a lot

TO A DEAR FRIEND

Kind eyes that penetrate the soul, and see therein
The secret that holds, with lips that are sealed
Kind heart who understands humanity, its pains, its fleeting joys
And one by one each burden unfolds
The travail of a heart that has touched the very depths
Are healed by your kind and sympathetic words
And in the broken mess of years, you draw out some thread of hope
Something that wasn't crushed or bruised through the conflicts of life
A mere speck, too small to trifle with
Yet your kind words, filled with years of experience
Fan it forth like a beacon to lead us on
Showing us the road of sacrifice leads to understanding
To appreciate more the goodness we
Carelessly took without a thought of payment
You taught me that life is but a give-and-take

TO J.M.V.

Even though I shall flit away on wings of love
Not caring of tomorrow
On my wild gypsy trail winding away unendingly
Loving you today, unmindful of tomorrow

I'll not wait till tomorrow
To tell you how much I care
I'll not wait till roses die
To start my dream again

But if tomorrow should come
I'll chant the same dear tune
Straight from my wild heart
Will come these tender words…I love you

TO W.B.

Why is it your eyes gleam tauntingly?
They're as cold as the sapphire sky on a winter morn
Like icicles glinting where warmth should be
Not a spark of laughter you have ever worn
Though sometimes your lips curve in a crooked grin
Not that softness that I often hope to see
But a ghastly grin, and its whiteness doesn't fail to show
The coldness that your heart hides within
I dare not ask…
But has someone taken the laughter from your eyes?
The softness that should have framed your smile?
Has Cupid's arrow shattered your dreams
That now you seem so reckless and wild?

TO MY MOTHER

To you, who went on uncomplaining
Marking your footsteps on the clay of life
For others, who in darkness
Shall be guided on the way
You taught me things I yet don't understand
How knowledge could be found on a flower
Or a star that shines above
Why every little river winding away unendingly
Can bring beauty
As in your eyes reveal
A light; in my heart a pang
For I still don't see
The beauty that your eyes don't conceal

THE TRAIL TO THE NORTHERN PINES

We don't envy those in the cities
With their skyscrapers and wide avenues,
Their palaces so fine, where they dance and dine to
    a lot of swing music and ballyhoo.
They have some grand old theaters—
We don't say that they can be beat;
And the stores where you buy your furs and toys
Will sweep you right off your feet.
Still, you may have the light and the glamour
That the cities can offer you,
But we'll follow the trail to the Northern Pines,
Where skies are azure blue.

The soft-patted trails 'neath the pine trees
Where no blast of a horn will you hear,
And the air is as clear as a crystal
And your friends are the four-footed deer,
Where you needn't do things in a hurry,
And your stride can be as lazy anytime,
For your heart is forever light and merry
On the trail to the Northern Pines.
When you feel a song coming on, you can sing it;
Why bother if your neighbor's humor fails?
You can yodel away throughout the day,
And you're sure not to wake up in jail.

You don't have to worry about the landlord;
He'd never think of bothering you any time,
For the rent is free when you live out in the breeze

On the trail to the Northern Pines.
You can forget a lot about your appearance;
Your legs needn't be a burden to your spine;
Barefooted on the shores
On the trail to the Northern Pines.

Let the wind comb your hair in the breeze,
For Mother Nature will stir your cheeks in bloom;
Come a sparkle in your eye and a song in your heart,
And your legs can dance a rhythm to a tune.

There won't be no ringing from a timepiece
To change your carefree humor to a scowl;
You can turn on your side till the sun shines high,
And not wake up when you hear the coyotes howl.
You don't have to take a dose of medicine
That the radio announcers advertise
About clearing your head and pep to your step,
And something about a twinkle in your eye.
They can brag a lot about its miracles
They guarantee to put you top shape anytime,
But the tonic that can cure your ailments and be sure
Is on the trail to the Northern Pines.

Hidden trails that you can tramp at leisure
Where the woodsy tang is heavy in the air,
And the birds will sing songs that'll give swing tunes the gong
To the graceful leap of a fleeting hare;
The stream where you won't lie about the big one
That got away with your rod and line,
For the whoppers you can catch will cover your bet
On the trail to the Northern Pines.
It's a place where you can relax again,
And forget about the things you left behind;

You're called Mister in the land, but here, you're just a man
On the trail to the Northern Pines.

UNTAMED

Alone…you love to ramble in the twilight
Beyond the moonlit hills
On to the silvery streams
Your graceful body, with its flowing curves
Enchants your loveliness
Beyond my wildest dreams
Though it's hard to tell from your silent lips
Or from your mysterious eyes
That gaze over the waves, rolling on eternally
That over there, beyond the deep, dark waters
A breath of wind carries a message of love
Unknowingly…from thy one immortally

UNTAMED LOVE

Why sit and dream of being what you want to be?
Pretending will not bring what you crave
Love might be sweet in dreams, sweeter than life could be
But that's all, unless you care to brave
The journey of carefree youth, taunting all who disapprove
Proving your freedom from all standards they built
Crushing them beneath your heel, with the undoubting recklessness of youth
Uncaring if there are offending snips, yet knowing you are untouched by guilt
You might yearn for the wildness of nature
Its rugged beauty calls to your innermost soul
Touched by the taint of the wilderness, its beauty unravels freedom in ecstasy
To banish that heartache longing, bravely to reach your goal
A gypsy at heart, in actions and deeds, untamed to the code of others
Dancing in the sunlight and moonlight, with the wild song throbbing from your heart
Lighted by that inspiration of unfathomed love, driving you on
To the very heights of timeless emotions, a call from heart to heart
In a fierce embrace, hot kisses find yielding lips in the magic spell of moonlight
No false morals to haunt and taunt you, no written code to answer to
Young love finds two wild lights in two eager, innocent eyes
The hot blush of two smooth young cheeks, and the wild thrill of soft, fragrant lips
Others dare not to contradict you, dare to interfere with their false morals of life
A love that had flamed to a burning adoration, and blessed by God above

Trusting and loyal, an unresisting sensation to the true, unwritten code

Youth, flaming youth…symbolizing the true, wild, untamed love

USELESS

I wish I could tell you the pain that's in my heart
The achingness of life without you
The terrible longing that's breaking my heart
And the weary hours I spend in solitude

What is the use of my loving, weaving dreams about you?
What is the use of my teardrops? It only makes me blue
I lie and dream and pretend that you're near
I kneel and pray, my eyes blinded with tears
But what is the use of my dreaming things that will never come true?

What is the use of pretending, when my heart knows the truth?

WHEN I THINK OF YOU

When the leaves come tumbling down
    And the autumn winds do blow
Scattering colors of red and gold
    On the painted ground below
It's when I think of you
    When the bare trees gently moan
As if lost ghosts are wandering through
    The darkened forest alone
It makes me wonder
    When skies are a pastel blue
When large, dark clouds go traveling over
    The purplish hills the sun once knew
If somewhere you are thinking
    Of harvest days gone by
When the moon did shine so tenderly
    And the stars were twinkling in the sky
It seems the same dear days are coming back
    When autumn comes around
Though it's all the same, but years are passing
    And the pal I had is gone
But no matter where you are tonight
    I love you, fond and true
And when the leaves come tumbling down
    That's when I most yearn for you

WHEN YOU'RE GONE

What will the years be when you're gone
When my anxious heart shall hear no more
Your familiar footsteps on the garden lane
And your hurried knock upon the door?
What will I do, dear, when evening steals
When your laughing eyes no more I see
Your winning smile that bought me joy
And your loving kiss that thrilled me?
Who will care, dear, when you're gone
When evening steals and lights are low
What my anguished heart cries out in pain
And from my blinded eyes tears flow?
I cannot bear what life will hold for me
When you're gone
My heart cries out: take me where you go
For darling, I can't here linger on

WHY

Why doesn't someone want to love me?
Why am I always feeling blue?
Tearfully, lonely, I'm here waiting,
Thinking, wondering, dreaming of you.
Anguished tears sparkle down my cheeks,
Like drops of fire burning my hand,
And that gnawing feeling that seems to tear at my heart
Is what? I cannot understand.

WHY THIS BRIEF STAY CALLED LIFE?

The goal was reached,
And still that happiness was not felt
That complete existence, a heaven of peace and contentment
That a life lived to the fullest can only reveal
But what have we when we reach the goal of our making?
Have we that complete feeling of satisfaction?
Or do we find, to our despair, a vague emptiness
Or something that was missed, of something that was left behind?
Or did we purposely fling it aside to achieve the ends of our own selfish desires?
We take from life only what we put in,
And life is but a brief stay, so fleeting, our destiny is not revealed until too late
The little things in life that we knowingly left behind
Come to the top to taunt us, to mock us and crush us
And in its awakening, we find a failure twice its capacity
We are but mortals struggling in the darkness
The light of ambition is the only beacon that leads us on
And if on the road of life it should dim, discouragement settles on our path
Where to turn in our despair? Only toward the master who watches over us
Who understands our yearnings and sees our blunders
It's placing our goal beyond death that will assure us of our success
It's the appreciation, the complete feeling of unselfish work done
That should mean more to us than its achievements
Ah! We are but victims of our own folly, our own individuality, our own conceit,
Into a hollow sphere we seem to be, and its escape is only death

To understand life is but to open the door to greatness
And to go on means self-abandon, sacrifices unselfishly done
Which at the end can only bring us the priceless gift: happiness

WILD DREAMS

Out in the starlight we stole, for a few wild moments of love
Though challenged youth bold, we dared not linger on
For eyes unseen were gazing through the dim, mystic gloom
But unheedingly, daring, we stole 'neath the moon
For it was our last night—oh, it was so brief
But I have one relief: though I'll be gone, your kisses will linger on
'Neath other skies we'll journey, through life's highways alone
Each undoubting…struggling on to our destinies…on…on
For these rare moments tender, dare not to trample on
But just to remember…when I'm gone
A grim consolation that wounds heal, but scars remain
To awaken again in memory love's sad refrain
Life goes on and on, but our minds stray back
If only for a brief instant, pretending is so sweet
To stray back in starlight…and again we'll meet

YESTERDAY

Still is the night without you
Memories drifting back
Leaves tumbling in the breeze
Seem to bring back to me
Each memory of yesterday
Each star shining in the sky
Knows that each sigh
Is a symbol of my love for you
Although you're far away
I'm drifting back again to yesterday

978-0-595-81081-9
0-595-81081-0

Printed in the United States
86462LV00004BG/1/A